15-minute focus
Brief Counseling
Techniques that Work

SUICIDE
PREVENTION,
INTERVENTION, AND
POSTVENTION

D1527911

NATIONAL CENTER for
YOUTH ISSUES

Duplication and Copyright

NCYI titles may be purchased in bulk at special discounts for
educational, business, fundraising, or promotional use. For more
information, please email sales@ncyi.org.

NATIONAL CENTER for
YOUTH ISSUES

P.O. Box 22185
Chattanooga, TN 37422-2185
423.899.5714 • 866.318.6294
fax: 423.899.4547 • www.ncyi.org

ISBN: 978-1-937870-75-1 $14.95
Library of Congress Control Number: 2020913562
© 2020 National Center for Youth Issues, Chattanooga, TN
All rights reserved.
Written by: Melisa Marsh
Published by National Center for Youth Issues
Starkey Printing • Chattanooga, TN, U.S.A.
September 2020

Contents

See page 63 for information about Downloadable Resources.

Introduction

Hope is a necessity for normal life and the major weapon against the suicide impulse.

—Karl. A. Menninger

When you ask most people what they think about suicide or even suicide prevention, you will get a variety of responses—sad, scary, heartbreaking. While all of these thoughts and feelings are absolutely true, they all have a negative connotation associated with them. I have a different perspective that I would like to share related to the work we can do with suicide and suicide prevention.

I come from a place of hope. I am hopeful that we can make a difference. I am hopeful that we can save a life. I am hopeful that we can impact the stigma that is associated with suicide and mental health. As you read this book, I hope that you will keep this idea in mind. I, too, know that suicide is heartbreaking. I am only here after many of my own professional and personal experiences with suicide. But after all of the dust settles, I am still hopeful because I know that there are those who also care and who want to also keep others safe.

This book is designed to not only share the stigma and data associated with suicide, but also to provide you with an implementable plan to make your community safer. Therefore, I will provide you with specific language to use when speaking about suicide, strategies related to suicide prevention, strategies related to suicide intervention, and strategies related to suicide postvention. I will also provide you with strategies that can be used with your administration, with your teachers, and in a virtual environment. Finally, you will find a series of resources that you can modify and implement in your school setting.

This book is for you. The support person who worries if you have done enough. The support person who moves heaven and earth to support individuals with thoughts of suicide. The support person who keeps yourself composed all day and then breaks down at night because the work is so exhausting physically, emotionally, and spiritually. I see you. I have been you. Stay hopeful, my friend. You are not alone in the work that you do. And together we will make a difference.

1 The Stigma

*What mental health needs is more sunlight,
more candor, more unashamed conversation.*

—Glenn Close

Suicide and suicidal ideation can be a complicated and heavy topic. Many schools and school districts are hesitant to directly discuss suicide with students for fear of associated stigma. I present all around the country on the topic of suicide prevention. I usually survey participants at the beginning of our time together to better know their needs so that our time together is meaningful. And I'll ask the following questions:

Does your district/school offer a suicide prevention program?

Does your district/school offer a suicide intervention program?

Does your district/school offer a suicide postvention program?

The data that I receive back from them is consistent across the country:

- About 48 percent of the participants respond that they do not have a suicide prevention program in place.
- About 44 percent of the participants respond that they do not have a suicide intervention program in place.
- About 59 percent respond that they do not have a suicide postvention program in place.

These numbers are terrifying, especially when we know that suicide is the second leading cause of death for people between the ages of ten and thirty-four.[1] What are we missing? Upon knowing this data, why are school districts still hesitant to put suicide programs in place? Part of it is due to stigma.

Oftentimes, individuals avoid talking about suicide out of fear that even saying the word could trigger a person to act on suicidal thoughts. However, research shows that this is not the case. According to a study published in *Psychological Medicine*, it is very difficult to implant the thought of suicide into someone's head when they have not already been thinking about the topic.[2] Interestingly enough, we as support staff often believe that it is others who have a difficult time talking about suicide. As I travel around the country to present on the topic of suicide prevention, I am still surprised at the number of school counselors, school social workers, school psychologists, administrators, teachers, and other staff members who are nervous to talk about suicide. Even asking them to say the word *suicide* out loud makes them uncomfortable. I am continuously asked if another word or phrase can be used. "Could we talk about hurting yourself instead?" is a common question that I receive. But the research clearly shows that we must be clear and direct when we are talking about suicide. Researchers looked at the concerns of talking to individuals about suicide and the impact that it had on them. The research showed that there was no increase in suicidal ideation when the participants were directly asked about suicide. In fact, there was a decrease, showing that talking directly about suicide "may lead to improvements in mental health treatment seeking populations."[3] Unfortunately, until we are willing and able to name it, say it, and discuss it, it will be challenging to remove the stigma.

Aside from the work that we need to do among our own support staff, there is a much broader level of reducing the stigma associated with suicide. According to research by The Center for Health Policy at the IU Richard M. Fairbanks School of Public Health, suicide has a high level of public stigma.

When addressing stigma at this level, the interventions must be intentionally focused on including public education campaigns that are "designed to provide the general public with evidence-based facts about the underlying causes of mental illness."[4] These types of campaigns would help to dispel misinformation and stereotypes about suicide or about individuals who suffer from thoughts of suicide, and they can be done at a district or a school-based level. They are appropriate for students, staff, families, and the greater community. There is evidence to support educational campaigns and the impact that they have on decreasing the stigma of suicide. One study conducted in Scotland that addressed the inaccurate portrayal of mental illness reported that educational campaigns are associated with a 17 percent decrease in the belief that individuals with mental illness are dangerous.[5] These continued efforts to educate our communities are another way that we can help to reduce the stigma that is still negatively impacting our work with suicide prevention.

A Student's Story

After experiencing a death by suicide that took place in our school community, I was meeting with a student who liked to speak with me about various aspects of his life. He was a very introspective young man who liked to ask questions about the world that surrounded him. On that particular day, the question that he posed to me was: "Do you think that students are really going to come and talk to adults if they are thinking about suicide?"

I was both a little hurt and shocked, but trying to show neither on my face. However, I was also intrigued, so I asked him what he meant by his question. He shared with me that if he were ever to think about suicide, he would not go talk to an adult but, instead, would more likely go to his peers. He found that, traditionally, teens trusted and confided in their peers more than adults. Adults would be more judgmental and not really understand the situation.

After processing the conversation for multiple days, and beginning to do some research, I realized that this student was right. Even if we built beautiful relationships with our students, they would likely go to a peer first to share their true feelings.

The next day my student returned and thanked me for allowing him to have such an honest conversation about suicide. He gifted me with the book *Thirteen Reasons Why* by Jay Asher.[6] At that time, it was just a book and not a popular series on Netflix. He encouraged me to read it and offered to talk about it. He shared that it was a book that many of the students were reading, and this was how they discussed suicide.

I did read the book, and we had many interesting conversations that followed this initial conversation. I will always be grateful to this young man for his bravery and his willingness to openly and honestly talk with me about suicide.

QUESTIONS to CONSIDER

1. Does your district/school offer a suicide prevention/ intervention/postvention program? If so, what does it look like?

2. Why do you feel some school districts are hesitant to put suicide programs in place?

3. Why are teachers and school administrators hesitant to talk directly about suicide with students?

KEY POINTS

- Many schools and school districts are hesitant to directly discuss suicide with students for fear that in just talking about it, students would act on suicidal thoughts.
- Suicide is the second leading cause of death for people between the ages of ten and thirty-four.[7]
- Research shows that there is no increase in suicidal ideation when participants are directly asked about suicide. In fact, there is a decrease.
- Educational campaigns that help dispel misinformation and stereotypes about mental illness can be done at a school or district level and can help reduce the stigma around suicide.

Terminology

Words have a magical power. They can bring either the greatest happiness or deepest despair.

—Sigmund Freud

Before we move any further, it is important to clarify some terminology that is critical to the suicide prevention process. Not only will you see it used throughout the book, but I want to ensure that you have a clear understanding of each term and the context. Think of this section as Suicide Vocabulary 101. *Suicide*, according to Merriam-Webster, is defined as the act of taking one's own life voluntarily and intentionally.

Let's start with how we talk about suicide. When a person completes the act of suicide, the most common phrase that I hear is "committed suicide." That terminology should no longer be used. While this may not seem like a big deal, take a moment and really think about the word *commit*. The term "committed suicide" is hurtful and damaging for a multitude of reasons. Many people associate "commit" with "committing a crime" or "committing a sin." Beyond that, it also ignores the fact that suicide is oftentimes linked to a mental illness, trauma, etc.[8] As discussed in the previous section, removing this terminology is also a step toward reducing the stigma associated with suicide.

Instead of using the phrases "committed suicide" or "commit suicide," we should use the phrases "died by suicide" or "suicided." Even as a trainer for suicide prevention, it took me a little while to change my vocabulary and adjust to these newer phrases. However, knowledge is the first step. Then, we should put that knowledge to practice by using these appropriate phrases in our conversations and trainings about suicide.

A few terms that you have already seen include prevention, intervention, and postvention. I want to give you a brief description of each term to ensure that we have the same understanding as we move forward in this work.

Suicide Prevention – What you put in place in your school or district to proactively diminish the risk of suicide. There are various research-based programs which I will discuss later in the book that are available as suicide prevention. There are also a few key terms associated with suicide prevention. These are:

> **Risk Factors:** Certain events and circumstances that may increase the risk for suicide. Examples include previous suicide attempt(s), history of suicide in the family, substance abuse, mood disorders, access to lethal means, losses in personal life, history of abuse or trauma, and so on.

> **Warning Signs:** Any indication that an individual may be experiencing depression or thoughts of suicide. Examples include changes in appearance, changes in sleep/appetite, increased irritability, decreased interest in usual activities, suicidal threats/notes, etc.

> **Protective Factors:** Personal traits or environmental qualities that can reduce the risk of mental illness and thoughts of suicide. Examples include strong problem-solving skills, positive self-image, spiritual faith, close family relations, strong peer support, etc.

Suicide Intervention – What you put in place in your school or district as a direct effort to prevent a person from attempting to take their own life. It is important to note that we often think of our students, but this also applies to our staff. Many times, people on staff have thoughts of suicide, but there is not a plan in place to support them. Again, there are various research-based programs I will discuss later that are available as suicide intervention.

Suicide Postvention – What you put in place in your school or district as an organized response in the aftermath of a suicide to facilitate healing, mitigate other negative effects, and prevent suicide among people who are at high risk after exposure to suicide. There is a gap in programming for suicide postvention. However, we will later discuss some best practices and ways to implement suicide postvention in your school and district.

Other phrases that I want to clarify before moving forward are the differences between an individual with thoughts of suicide (also known as suicide ideation), having a suicide plan, and making a suicide attempt. These three phrases are used together very often in the suicide intervention stage; however, they have very different meanings and levels of severity. An individual who has thoughts of suicide or suicidal ideation is exploring the idea of suicide. At this stage they have formed ideas about taking their own life. When a person has a suicide plan, they know the means that they would use to take their own life. They may or may not have access to these means, but they have developed a way that they would complete the suicide. Finally, the individual who has attempted suicide has actively tried to end their life. As mentioned previously, when discussing any of these terms, we want to practice using the correct terminology as a way to model for others as well as build relationships with those who are experiencing thoughts of suicide.[9]

A Student's Story

When a student dies by suicide, it is normal to retrace all of the events, actions, and moments leading up to the death. What were the risk factors? What were the warning signs? What were the protective factors? Why was I not more in tune to the social and emotional needs of this young person? There are so many emotions that are involved for those who are left behind.

During the aftermath of a death by suicide, I was contacted directly by the family and invited to their home. Although the young man who died was not my student, I had formed a close relationship with the family over the years because their eldest daughter attended my high school. After much consultation with my principal, we decided that the social worker and I would both go to the home to support the family at their request.

I remember entering their home and feeling so helpless. What could I offer to a mother, father, and daughter who had just lost their son or brother? But I focused on my training and was determined to be the constant professional and support this grieving family. They had similar questions to those I had been asking myself: what were the warning signs?

In leaving the home that afternoon, the mom gave me a hug and thanked me for joining them. She shared that it was the first time that her daughter had spoken about her feelings since her brother's death. At that moment I realized that it was not only about what I was doing for her in that moment, but about what we had built over time. It was about our relationship.

QUESTIONS to CONSIDER

1. Why is the phrase "committed suicide" hurtful and damaging?

2. What phrases should be used instead?

3. What are the differences between an individual with thoughts of suicide, having a suicide plan, and making a suicide attempt?

KEY POINTS

- Removing incorrect terminology about suicide helps reduce the stigma surrounding it.
- Suicide Prevention is what you put in place in your school or district to reduce the risk of suicide.
- Suicide Intervention is what you put in place in your school or district to prevent a person from attempting to take their own life.
- Suicide Postvention is what you put in place in your school or district as an organized response in the aftermath of a suicide.

3 **By the Numbers**

If we have data, let's look at data.
If all we have are opinions, let's go with mine.
—Jim Barksdale

Before we can implement suicide prevention programs, suicide intervention programs, or suicide postvention programs, we must look at the data. Schools and districts are not going to simply implement programs because I ask them to or you ask them to. After all, we have already established that there is a stigma and fear around the concept of suicide. Therefore, we must show them the numbers. Data does not lie. Earlier, I shared with you some of the data that I have collected across the country related to schools and districts that do not have these programs. Now we need to focus on why school districts need to implement programs that will support individuals who experience thoughts of suicide.

Let's begin by looking at some of the basics. As I've already mentioned, suicide is the second leading cause of death for individuals from ages ten to thirty-four.[10] It's also the tenth leading cause of death in the United States.[11] In 2018, 48,344 Americans died by suicide, and these were only the reported cases.[12] It is important to note that while this data is the most accurate data that has been reported, researchers believe that the suicide rates are actually higher. This is most commonly due to underreporting based on stigma. According to the CDC, we have seen a 33 percent increase in the suicide rate from 1999 to 2017.[13] What is specifically interesting about this increase is that it does not discriminate based on race, sex, age, etc. All of our demographics are increasing.

Now, let's look specifically at the data for our student populations. While they are also showing an increase, the data reveals more. According to the Center for Disease Control, 31.6 percent of our students nationwide have felt so sad or hopeless almost every day for two or more weeks that they stopped doing some of their usual activities, which indicates that they may be experiencing a form of depression.[15] Also, 17.2 percent of our students shared that they were seriously considering attempting suicide, 13.6 percent of our students made a suicide plan, and 7.4 percent of our students attempted suicide.[16] If you are anything like me, arbitrary numbers don't work as well as specifics. Let's look at a graduating class with five hundred students. I realize this might be small for some of your schools and huge for others, but it is a good average. If 17.2 percent of a graduating class of five hundred had thought about or were thinking about suicide, that would mean eighty-six of your students. Then, if 13.6 percent of the class had made a suicide plan, that would be sixty-eight students. Finally, if 7.4 percent of the graduating class had attempted suicide, that would be thirty-seven students. What would an average day or week look like if this was the case at your school? How busy would you be? Do you have the resources to support these students? Just think about it.

We know that, according to the data, the suicide rate continues to increase. Why? According to Christine Moutier, doctor and chief medical officer of the American Foundation for Suicide Prevention, there is no simple answer. She says, "At the individual level, there is never a single cause of suicide. There are always multiple risk factors."[17] That being said, we can see trends in the data both in the United States as well as in other nations around the world. These trends lend insights into part of the puzzle regarding the uptick in the suicide data.

Socioeconomic changes seem to have a direct correlation with the suicide data trends. In a study conducted by Dr. Anne Case and Dr. Angus Deaton, they demonstrated that when living conditions improve, the suicide rates fall. Unfortunately, the reverse occurs when living conditions worsen.[18] During periods of hardship, individuals who are struggling often lose the resources and interventions that could be the most helpful in preventing suicide. According to Moutier, the mental health care system has not been designed with suicide prevention in mind. It is neither accessible nor affordable.[19]

Aside from socioeconomic factors, we must also remember all of the risk factors that come into play with suicide. As noted in our terminology section, risk factors include depression, mental illness, physical health conditions, stressful life events such as relationship problems, and so on. While these factors alone do not indicate that a person is suicidal, they can be stress-inducing and challenging for anyone to handle. When I do trainings, I like to talk about these factors by introducing three categories:

1. **Groups of People Who Might Be at Risk for Thoughts of Suicide**

   We must ask the question: who are the individuals who are at a higher risk for having thoughts of suicide? Examples might be those who have previously attempted suicide, the LGBTQ community, someone who just lost a loved one, someone suffering from depression, and so on.

2. **Events**

   What are stressful events in life? Examples might be a divorce, a death, failing grades, bad health, etc.

3. **Reactions**

   What are some reactions that we might have to these events? For example, we might feel sad, we might feel alone, we might start to experiment with drugs or alcohol, we might stay out too late, etc. I ask the participants to make the lists in each of the categories (at-risk people, events, and reactions), then I follow up with an activity.

I ask my participants: "Could an individual in the LGBTQ community who just lost a loved one and is experimenting with alcohol be someone who is thinking about suicide?" Basically, I have taken one item from each of the three groups and put them together. The participants always say yes.

Then I give them another example, "Could an individual who has previously attempted suicide, who is going through a divorce, and might have stayed out too late have thoughts of suicide?" Again, the participants answer yes. Then I change the question. "But, do they *have* to be experiencing thoughts of suicide?" There is usually a pause in the room, followed by one voice that says no. "Why not?" I ask. Participants will answer to this effect: "Because these are just indications that they *could* have thoughts of suicide." I ask, "And what is it that really determines whether or not they have thoughts of suicide?" Again, there is always a pause here. Then someone will eventually say, "It is the individual's *reaction* to these events."

While we can't know for certain why our data continues to increase, we have some very good predictors. In the meantime, we are able to determine risk factors. And not only can we determine the risk factors, but we can teach individuals how to develop coping skills and techniques to respond to these risk factors so that their reaction does not overwhelm them. This is work that you are hopefully already doing in your programs, and, if not, then you need to think about how you can incorporate teaching developmentally appropriate coping skills, anger management, and other techniques that help individuals focus on their reaction.

A Student's Story

Sometimes we don't learn the story until it is too late. I recently attended a crisis response for a young lady who died by suicide. From the school's perspective, they knew that she had some grades that were slipping, and she was on probation from being in the Magnet program in the high school. While this was a challenge, the rest of her high school world seemed to be intact.

After the death, her mother shared with the school that she and her husband had recently caught her with drugs in the home. She had received strong disciplinary consequences, which caused a tension-filled life in their home environment. We were now beginning to see a compounding story for a young lady who was struggling at school and at home.

Finally, after her death, her friends shared that her boyfriend, who attended college, had died by suicide two weeks earlier. The young lady was devastated and felt alone and isolated. While her friends tried to console her, she continued to withdraw from them more each day. We were then able to see the story of a young lady who was struggling in school and at home and was feeling completely isolated. She already thought suicide was an option based on the death of her boyfriend.

After putting the full story together, the guilt was compounding. Would the outcome have been different if these groups had communicated their concerns? This is why it is so critical that all groups know the signs of suicide and understand the importance of speaking up when they have a concern.

QUESTIONS to CONSIDER

1. Who are the individuals who are at a higher risk for having thoughts of suicide?

2. What are some stressful events in life that could factor into suicide?

3. What are some reactions that students might have to these stressful events?

4. What should students, staff, and families do when they recognize signs of suicide in another individual?

KEY POINTS

• Suicide is the second leading cause of death for individuals from ages ten to thirty-four[20] and the tenth leading cause of death in the United States.[21] And, according to data, the suicide rate continues to increase.

• There are multiple risk factors when it comes to suicide: depression, mental illness, physical health conditions, stressful life events such as relationship problems, and so on.

• We must learn to recognize people who are at higher risk of suicide and teach them coping skills and techniques.

Suicide Prevention Strategies for School Counselors and Support Staff

Never, never, never give up.
—Winston Churchill

As caregivers, you have an innate desire to help others. You might see this in your personal life as well as in your professional life. Occasionally, a problem arises where you may not know how to help. I find this to be the case when people begin to talk about suicide. In the next few sections of this book, I am going to provide you with a variety of strategies and resources that can be implemented in your school and district. It is important to note that each of you has a set of guidelines that you must adhere to based on where you work. This is true for the public and the private school sector. Therefore, it is critical that before you try to implement any programs, policy changes, or processes, you review the rules and regulations of your environment.

My personal background is from a public school setting in two very large districts. In order to implement programs and changes in my buildings and in my district, I needed to review board policies, get approval from my principal (on a school level), work with my director and assistant superintendent (on a district level), and remember to collaborate with others who also valued the work. I would not have been able to implement changes in the school setting without the partnerships with my school social worker, my school psychologist, my entire counseling team, my principal, our teachers, and many others. Additionally, I would not have been able to implement changes in the district setting without partnerships with other supervisors (social work, psychology, and nursing), my coordinator of crisis coordination, my director, my assistant superintendent, and so many others who not only gave their feedback to the process, but then also assisted with the rollout. I mention this because we must always remember that we are not doing this work in isolation. You must have a team around you to share the vision, to share the hope, and to share the work. Together is the only way that we will be able to keep our students and our staff safe from suicide.

In this section, we are going to specifically focus on suicide prevention. As I mentioned earlier, when I survey individuals across the country, about 48 percent of the participants indicate that they do not have a suicide prevention program in their school or district. As a school counselor, I, too, fell into that 48 percent. I worked at a large, metro area school where the focus was on success—success in academics, success in the arts, and success in sports. There was not a large focus, at the time, on mental health and wellness, and most adults in the building and in the community were not willing to talk about these topics. One year, during our needs assessment with the community, my team was excited to see that there were families who had specifically asked for more resources and information on mental health. We were thrilled. My team worked diligently to plan for a community-wide event on the topic of mental wellness. We had a locally recognized expert as our speaker, we provided a number of breakout sessions for families to attend, and we advertised it in many ways to our surrounding community. When we arrived that evening, we were devastated to see that we had one parent attend the event. One! Our school alone had a population of about 2,500 students, so this showed us that although the families indicated that they were noticing a need for these services, they were not going to attend an event. The stigma was too great. The thinking was: "That's okay for other families, but not for mine." We knew we needed to change our perspective. How could we serve our community without making families feel like all eyes were on them? How could we truly serve all of our students and families? Unfortunately, we did not have much time to plan before our situation changed drastically.

That was the beginning of my hardest year as a school counselor. Once you have been in the profession for a while, you learn that certain years, months, or moments will change you forever. This was mine. We had five deaths in that single year. Yes, that is correct. Five. Those of you who have been through a single death of a student or staff member understand the impact that is felt by the whole community. However, with each additional death, it is compounded. We had our first death by suicide. The community was shocked and looking for answers. There were none to be found. The second death was a beloved faculty member who lost their battle with cancer. This loss impacted the community at large due to this individual's presence within the school community. The third death was another death by suicide. At this point, the community was beginning to grow concerned of the contagion effect. However, there was no indication that this death was related to our first loss. The fourth death was another death by suicide of a former student who had just recently graduated. After this loss, the community began to really focus on what we could do. We started seeing coalitions forming, PTSA wanting to provide supports, etc. Finally, the fifth death was another death by suicide of a former student who had graduated a few years earlier.

I share this with you for a few reasons. I want you to know that I have been there. I have seen the dark days of suicide, and I have walked in your shoes. I have also known how frustrating it can be to watch loss after loss without getting the support and changes you need. Throughout the whole year, my team continued to ask for additional resources, support, etc. Sometimes it felt like we were making headway, and other times it felt like we were hitting a dead end. But I also want you to know that you are stronger than you think you are. You have more grit and resilience than you realize. During that year, I thought I could not survive another day, another loss, another moment of trying to support students, staff, and families who were broken by the losses in our community. But each day, I would find enough strength to lead my team and comfort those in need.

In January of that year, after multiple losses, we were finally given a suicide prevention program to implement within our community. This is one of the prevention programs that I am sharing with you as a resource. It was a game changer for our school at that time, and I still use it with my district today. Before I share that resource with you, I want to give you a few guidelines for selecting a suicide prevention program for your school or district. First, I encourage you to look for evidence-based prevention programs. The Suicide Prevention Resource Center supports evidence-based programs, as they are more likely to reduce suicidal thoughts and behaviors.[22] Second, make sure that any program you select aligns with your school and district strategic plan and long-term goals.[23] Finally, use culturally competent approaches that can demonstrate effectiveness across diverse populations.[24]

The Suicide Prevention Resource Center is a great tool if you are looking for a suicide prevention program but don't know where to start. The website is: https://www.sprc.org/keys-success/evidence-based-prevention. On this page, you will find information related to planning, selecting a prevention program, developing interventions, and evaluation. In selecting a suicide prevention program, I would also recommend that you and your team consider selecting a program that includes students, staff, families, and the greater community. As I mentioned earlier, suicide prevention is not a one-person (or one-team) job. The more groups that are involved with and exposed to the program, the better it will help to communicate the message of suicide prevention.

Once you and your team have selected a suicide prevention program for your school or district, it is critical that you take time during the planning stages to thoroughly review all of the materials, plan your implementation, look for potential problems, and communicate clearly to everyone who will be involved in the rollout. Research shows that there are few programs that last for a long period of time in institutional settings (schools included). However, there are strategies that you can put in place to help increase the likelihood that the program you select will be effective.[25]

1. You must have the support of your administration. Many of the suicide prevention programs will ask for passive consent, time for classroom lessons, and distribution of prevention materials. Without the support of your administration, the program cannot be successful.[26]

2. You need to identify who is going to be responsible. While this is a team initiative, someone must take the lead. Who will that be? Who will do the set-up, the coordination, and the communication to ensure that the program rolls out effectively?[27]

3. Be prepared to provide ongoing consultation and support. As we previously discussed, talking about suicide makes individuals nervous. Your team needs to be prepared to talk about the program that is selected, provide ongoing support as needed, and constantly consult with staff, families, and students.[28]

I will always be grateful for the suicide prevention program that we were able to implement that year. After a full year of implementation, and continued use since that time, the school has data to support the evidence-based suicide prevention program and the impact it can have on a community.

Suicide Prevention Programs for Schools

The following programs, with the exception of one, are evidence-based suicide prevention programs for schools. Again, it is important to find the program that is the best fit for your school or district. I must note that many of these programs are for middle and high school students, as it can be very challenging to find a suicide prevention program for elementary-aged students. The last resource in this list is a children's book that can be used when conducting classroom lessons with elementary-aged students on the topic of suicide.

- **Signs of Suicide (SOS) Prevention Program** — Signs of Suicide (SOS) teaches students how to identify signs of depression and suicide in themselves and their peers, while training school professionals, parents, and community members to recognize at-risk students and take appropriate action. Using SOS, 90 percent of schools have seen an increase in students seeking help for themselves or a friend, with 95 percent believing the program also reduced stigma in schools. (middle school and high school)

- **Sources of Strength** — Sources of Strength provides the highest quality evidence-based prevention for suicide, violence, bullying, and substance abuse by training, supporting, and empowering both peer leaders and caring adults to impact their world through the power of connection, hope, help, and strength. (elementary school, middle school, and high school)

- **More Than Sad** — More Than Sad teaches teens to recognize the signs of depression in themselves and others, challenges the stigma surrounding depression, and demystifies the treatment process. (high school)

- **The Trevor Project** — Founded in 1998 by the creators of the Academy Award-winning short film *Trevor*, The Trevor Project is the leading national organization providing crisis intervention and suicide prevention services to lesbian, gay, bisexual, transgender, queer, and questioning (LGBTQ) young people under age twenty-five. The Lifeguard Workshop is a free online learning module for middle school and high school classrooms. The Trevor Project's trainings also include in-person Ally and CARE trainings designed for adults who work with youth. (middle school and high school)

- **A Flicker of Hope** — *A Flicker of Hope* is a book written by Julia Cook. When I was looking for developmentally appropriate suicide prevention programs for elementary school students, I was at a loss. But then I found this magical book. Julia is able to talk about difficult topics in a way that younger students can understand and feel safe. Sometimes you have to think outside the box and develop lessons based on the needs of your students. My district has developed a lesson to pair with *A Flicker of Hope* that is implemented with our elementary school students. (Please note this is not evidence-based).

A Staff Member's Story

I was ready to implement my first suicide prevention program in our high school. The kickoff event was going to be a training with all of our staff members during pre-planning. It was critical that all of the staff were familiar with the program, the data associated with suicide, and signs of suicide. I had been preparing and practicing for weeks, and I felt confident with the material. Although, honestly, I was also very nervous to be speaking publicly about suicide. This was my first time to speak to a group of individuals about suicide, and I had to practice more than usual due to the nature of the material.

The event started, and the presentation went very well. Then I showed a brief video to accompany my talk and personalize the information. When the video ended and the lights of the auditorium rose, I found my colleagues with a mixture of reactions. Some were crying, some were in shock, and some looked confused. The hands began to slowly rise. Are those our students? Do we really have students who think about suicide? What do we need to do? The video had made the data become real to the staff. They were now thinking about the students in their rooms and they were ready to make a difference.

Prior to the training, I felt like the school counselors were going to be doing this work alone. However, after the training, I realized that all of the staff was able to understand the importance of this work. They were ready to be part of the team that would help create a suicide safe community for our students.

QUESTIONS to CONSIDER

1. From what people do you need support in order to implement a suicide prevention program? List each person and their role.

2. Who will take the lead in rolling out the program? Who will do the set-up, the coordination, and the communication in the roll-out?

3. What are some reactions that students might have to these stressful events?

KEY POINTS

- Partnering with administrators, school counselors, and other support staff is critical to the work of suicide prevention.

- It is important to choose a suicide prevention program that is evidence-based, aligns with your school's and district's goals, and is culturally relevant among diverse populations.

- The program you choose should include students, staff, families, and the greater community. The more people involved with and exposed to the program, the better you can communicate the message of suicide prevention.

Suicide Intervention Strategies for School Counselors and Support Staff

The way I see it, if you want the rainbow,
you gotta put up with the rain.

—Dolly Parton

Suicide intervention is what support staff are most familiar with. Unfortunately, we see this too often in the school setting. A student comes to us, or is brought to us, because they are expressing thoughts of suicide. At that point, we intervene with the individual. I would like to encourage you to ask yourself: what does your intervention process look like? How are you truly serving your students during this intervention stage, and is it effective? Do you have evidence to support your work?

As I travel across the country and survey counselors and support staff, here is what a typical school process looks like:

The Process

1. A student expresses thoughts of suicide. This is then reported to the point of contact in the building—usually the school counselor.

2. The student is asked about their suicidal ideation, usually using a school or district protocol (if available). These

protocols typically include questions about the ideation, the plan, and the means.

3. Finally, if it is a serious threat, the student is monitored until they leave school. The family is contacted to pick up the student as soon as possible. If the case is very serious, emergency response may also be contacted.

Counselors are doing what they can to bring awareness to the family and get them to outside providers. However, there is a fear that there will not be follow-through when the student leaves the building. This process is not evidence-based, and aside from reporting the number of students who experience the various stages of suicide, it is very difficult to collect data.

This typical school process is not surprising as suicide training is not a large focus in many school counselor education programs. Most school counselors do not receive suicide training until they are in their practicums or internships, while others do not receive suicide training until they are in the field.[29] Most of us are trained on the job to save the lives of our students or staff who are experiencing thoughts of suicide.

I, too, fell into this category. I was not formally trained on suicide interventions until long into my career. I went through many years implementing the steps that I hear countless counselors and support staff share with me when they are describing their suicide intervention process. But then I realized I was missing a critical step in the process. What I used to do—and what many of us are currently doing—is upon hearing that there is a thought of suicide, I'd ask some formulaic questions and then tell the individual to sit there while we get in touch with their family. What must that feel like for the person with thoughts of suicide? They just shared that they are thinking about ending their life with you, and then they are asked to sit there and wait. You might be the only person they have ever shared this with. Can you imagine? What must they be feeling? Why do they want to die? What brought them to this place? And why would we leave them alone to wait while we contact their family instead of truly taking the time to listen to them?

This is the part of suicide intervention that we are missing. Dr. Ron Diamond, a professor of psychiatry at the University of Wisconsin School of Medicine and Public Health, shares that allowing people to talk about their suicidal thoughts is the first step to healing.[30] In a recent study published in the *Journal of General Internal Medicine*, a team completed semi-structured interviews with patients who had recently completed a questionnaire about self-harm and suicide. The patients who were selected for this study had selected that they had thoughts of suicide. During the interviews, all of the patients believed that being asked questions about their thoughts of suicide was appropriate. The direct communication with these trusted providers, who listened, helped to develop empathy and create comfort and additional disclosure.[31] Therefore, instead of asking someone to sit and wait after they share their thoughts about suicide, we should listen to their story. This is a great way to build rapport, provide empathy, and possibly determine some protective factors that might help them find a reason to live.

As in the previous section, there are also evidence-based suicide intervention models. I can personally tell you that after being trained in a suicide intervention model, I will never return to the "sit and wait" method ever again. Remember, it is critical that you carefully select the program that is the best fit for your school or district; there is no "one size fits all" in the world of education and definitely not in the world of suicide prevention and intervention. Below are some resources for your work during the suicide intervention stage of the process.

- **Applied Suicide Intervention Suicide Training (ASIST)** — *ASIST* is a two-day workshop designed for members of all caregiving groups. The emphasis is on teaching suicide first-aid to help an at-risk person stay safe and seek further help as needed. Participants learn to use a suicide intervention model to identify persons with thoughts of suicide, seek a shared understanding of reasons for dying and living, develop a safe plan based upon a review of risk, are prepared to do follow-up, and become involved in suicide-safer community networks.

- **Safety Planning** — A safety plan is a prioritized written list of coping strategies and sources of support developed by the counselor or support staff in collaboration with the individual who is experiencing thoughts of suicide. Safety planning incorporates elements of four evidence-based suicide risk reduction strategies:

  - Reducing access to lethal means
  - Teaching brief problem-solving and coping skills
  - Enhancing social support and identifying emergency contacts
  - Using motivational enhancement to increase likelihood of engagement in further treatment

It is important to note that these options do not have to be used in isolation. You can be ASIST trained and also implement safety plans. Layering is often done to ensure the safety of the individual with thoughts of suicide.

At this point in the suicide response process, you have heard the thoughts of suicide, you have listened to the story of the individual with thoughts of suicide, you have assessed the risk, and you have collectively created a safety plan. You are now ready to contact the family or emergency contact. As a caregiver, I know that can be a difficult call to make. However, I know it must be far worse to be on the receiving end of that call. If you have ever received a call like this, I can only imagine the panic and shock that must flow through every fiber of your being. That is why I suggest making the process as simple as possible for family members by supplying them with a conference summary. This is essentially a document for the family member that provides them with:

1. An outline of everything that was discussed on the call
2. What they need to do to keep their student safe
3. Next steps
4. A section that can be completed by a practitioner if they take their child for an assessment

A copy of this document is provided in the resource section of this book for your review. We have found that it is very helpful for families and also for the school counselors, as it gives them a guide to work through with the family, which serves as a checklist for them in a high-stress situation. Once the family has been contacted, you will want to communicate with your administration. Let them know the situation and the plan moving forward; some might even want a copy of the safety plan.

Finally, when the student returns to your school or district, I suggest implementing a re-entry plan. As a best practice, this would be a meeting that is conducted prior to the student arriving in the building. You would want to invite the teachers, possibly the nurse, the administrator, and anyone else who has regular contact with the student. The purpose of the meeting is to put any supports in place—whether academic or personal—that might be needed to help the student successfully transition back into the building. Some of the specific things you will want to cover are:

- Current medical care and updated medical documentation
- Process for make-up work and assignments
- Plan for how the student will answer questions from peers
- The Student Safety Plan if it needs any updating

Again, I will provide a copy of this document in the resource section for your review. We have found that it helps relieve stress for the families and students upon their return to the building. Additionally, it is helpful for all of the involved staff so that everyone is on the same page and can support students who have experienced this trauma.

A Student's Story

As school counselors and support staff, I feel certain that each of you can think of at least one student who has shared that they are thinking about suicide. Then, when you called the family to share the information, you were met with resistance, lack of belief, and no sense of urgency.

I had a young man who fit this description. He would come to me, share his thoughts of suicide, share his suicide plan, and then tell me that his family would not believe him. Sure enough, each time I would call his parents and express my concerns with them, and they would tell me to send him back to class, tell me that they don't believe him, and let me know that they would not be taking him to get any professional assistance.

After this happened twice, I went to my principal to let him know that I was greatly concerned for the young man and was going to make a report to DFCS for medical neglect. Our protocol advised to wait until the third time, but something in my gut told me that this young man needed immediate help. My principal was very supportive, and I moved forward with filing the DFCS report.

The next day the young man was back in school. As was my practice, I reached out to him to provide a checkpoint. The student again shared with me that he was experiencing thoughts of suicide. He then said that he could not take it any longer and went running out of my office. I followed him as quickly as I could. When I stepped in the hallway, he was sitting on the banister just outside of our counseling suite screaming that he was going to jump. Our counseling suite was on the third floor, and he would have been jumping down to the first floor.

I immediately froze. I didn't want to get too close to him, but I also wanted him to get down from the banister. Other students and staff began to come into the hallway due to his screaming. I signaled to a teacher to get help, which she immediately did.

Luckily, after about three minutes, he climbed down and walked back into the office.

This time when I called his parents it was with an administrator and the resource officer. They were told that due to the incident at school, the young man was a threat to himself. Therefore, they could either immediately come to the school and take him for an evaluation or we would be taking him to the hospital in an ambulance. The family finally realized the severity of the situation and got the help their son needed.

QUESTIONS to CONSIDER

1. What does your current intervention process look like? When a student shares that they are having thoughts of suicide, what steps do you take to address the situation?

2. How are you serving your students during this intervention stage, and is it effective?

3. Do you have evidence to support your work?

KEY POINTS

- A critical part of suicide intervention that we are missing is taking the time to truly listen to people's stories. Our first step should not be to have the student sit and wait while we call a parent or guardian.

- Once you have listened to the student's story, then you can contact the family or emergency contact. Afterwards, you should provide them a conference summary that includes what was discussed on the call, what they need to do to keep their student safe, next steps, and information to be completed by a practitioner.

- Finally, you should implement a re-entry plan for the student and staff. This meeting should take place prior to the student's return to school and should include updating medical documentation, a process for make-up work, a plan for how the student will answer any questions, and updating The Student Safety Plan.

Suicide Postvention Strategies for School Counselors and Support Staff

I breathe in my courage. I exhale my fear.

—Jonathan Huie

I truly believe that once you are touched by suicide, you are changed forever. A death by suicide has long-term and lasting implications that reach out like waves in the ocean; we cannot see their depth, their width, and all that are affected by their presence. Therefore, experiencing a death by suicide can be a major stressor, which increases the risks of social, physical, and mental health problems in addition to potential suicidal behaviors in the bereaved individuals.[32,33] Research shows that the impact of suicide, on average, will impact five immediate family members and up to 135 individuals.[34,35]

Many of us were taught the five stages of grief that were developed by Elisabeth Kubler-Ross: 1) denial, 2) anger, 3) bargaining, 4) depression, and 5) acceptance. While these stages are not linear, we are likely to see the bereaved experience varying degrees of these common grief reactions. It is also important to note that individuals who have experienced suicide may also be likely to experience shock or trauma related to the unexpected nature of the death. Many times, these individuals demonstrate feelings of abandonment, rejection, and shame, and they struggle to make meaning of the death.[36] Grief can be expressed in many ways, but it is important to remember that grief is a journey over time. It will change over time, but it does not end. We, as caregivers in the schools and in the school districts, should work toward reconciliation and not recovery for our bereaved. To do this there must be a concerted provision of support.

Throughout the years, various forms of postvention services have been developed, including grief counseling, group work, outreach by outside agencies, and online support.[37] Some of these services have been specifically focused and designed for a school setting.[38] I am always hopeful that most schools and districts have a suicide postvention program in place; however, based on the anecdotal data that I have collected, about 59 percent of the respondents we surveyed indicated that this is not the case. When a crisis occurs, schools are viewed by both students and families as a place to turn to for help and support. Therefore, schools and districts must be prepared to support the needs of their community. In this chapter, I will provide you with some best practices for developing a suicide postvention program. As I mentioned in the previous sections, you must think about the demographics and needs of your school and your district. Additionally, you must ensure that you are adhering to all of your policies, procedures, and practices that outline the requirements for your setting. There is not a "one size fits all" when dealing with suicide.

The first step to suicide postvention is to create and implement a response plan. This needs to be a well-developed plan that is communicated to the staff on a regular basis, where each staff member knows their role, and that can be activated at a moment's notice. Here are some logistical suggestions that can assist in a smooth response plan. Making these arrangements prior to the beginning of the school year is invaluable to your suicide postvention throughout the year.

1. Develop a staff phone tree/messaging system.

2. Identify a location for both student support and staff support (separate locations). Keep supplies on hand for your care centers. Examples would include tissues, water, art supplies, a stack of passes, sign-in materials, light refreshments, etc.

3. Prepare a list of home/cell phone numbers for support personnel.

During this developmental stage, it is helpful to have a description of each team member's role and responsibility. I also suggest that the local school team meet regularly to review the protocol that is developed. This is the only way that you will be the most prepared when grief comes to your school. In the resources section, you will find a series of items that you can use as a template for your suicide postvention, including a manual, roles and responsibilities, and a checklist.

Once your school or district has a response plan in place for a death by suicide, you will then need to implement your suicide postvention plan. This is always going to be a challenging day no matter how well-prepared you are. However, being prepared will give you and your team the confidence to know that you are ready and able to serve the students, families, and community to the best of your ability. Here are some suggestions to make that process run as smoothly as possible.

1. **Designate a media contact.** (This is usually the principal or their designee.)

2. **Confirm and prepare a written statement regarding the facts of the death.**

   It is critical to ensure that prior to giving out any information regarding the student or staff member the family or the police have confirmed the cause of death. With a death by suicide, due to stigma, sometimes the family does not want to release this information publicly.

3. **Hold a faculty meeting prior to the beginning of the school day and at the end of the school day.**

It is also a best practice to contact any staff that directly works with the student in advance to let them know personally.

It is rarely a good idea to announce the death over the loudspeaker, as this can cause hysteria and a large exodus from class.

4. **Be clear with your care center procedures.**
5. **Prepare a letter to send to the community.**

Again, I am including examples of these items (the letters, the scripts for speaking to classrooms, etc.) in the resource section for easy reference. Please remember that not all of these items are the responsibility of the school counselor or support staff; some of these would be conducted by your principal/headmaster. However, they may rely on you to support them through this process. In the year that I described to you, my year with the five deaths, my principal and I worked hand-in-hand after each loss. I would meet him in his office early in the morning to review our plan. We would contact the teachers who were directly connected to the student, plan what to share at the faculty meeting, map out the plan for our care rooms, and work on the scripts and letters together. I was able to rely on my counseling team, school social worker, school psychologist, and the crisis team who came from other buildings to oversee the care rooms so that I could be the "coordinator" for the day and ensure that everything was managed as it needed to be. This is why it is critical to determine roles. You need to know your team, the strengths and weaknesses, and determine each role so that the students and staff receive the support that is needed.

A Student's Story

Processing grief can be one of the hardest things we do as humans, but it can also be one of the most beautiful things to watch occur. The way people come together to love, honor, and support one another during a loss is truly inspiring and can provide hope in a very difficult situation.

After the death of a student, I went out to the school as part of the crisis team. We knew that this loss was going to be particularly hard on the community as the student was a well-loved, very involved senior. We also had two other crises that were going on in the school district, so our crisis support team was somewhat smaller than we would have preferred it to be for a student death.

The crisis team and local school counselors had a wonderful plan, and executed it well. Classes, students, and staff were supported throughout the day. However, students continued to pour into the crisis center. They needed more than the usual support; they needed to truly process and share with one another.

We asked the students to get in a circle and asked our crisis coordinator, who is trained in restorative practices, to help the students share their experiences. This was exactly what they needed. They had a chance to laugh. They had a chance to cry. They had a chance to connect with one another. But mostly, they had a chance to mourn the loss of their friend.

1. What are the five stages of grief?

2. What are some feelings students can have after a death by suicide of one of their classmates?

3. Why is it important not to announce the death over a loudspeaker at school?

4. Why is it critical to assign roles for everyone involved in your suicide postvention plan?

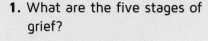

KEY POINTS

• The first step to suicide postvention is to create and implement a response plan that includes a staff phone tree/messaging system, separate care centers for student and staff support with necessary supplies (tissues, water, refreshments, art supplies, etc.), and a list of phone numbers for support personnel.

• The second step to suicide postvention is to implement your suicide postvention plan. Here, you will need to designate a media contact, prepare a written statement regarding the facts of the death, hold a faculty meeting prior to the school day and at the end of the school day, be clear with your care center procedures, and prepare a letter to send to the community.

Suicide P/I/P Strategies for Administrators

Crisis forces commonality of purpose on one another.

—Michelle Dean

There is a beautiful dance that happens between school counselors/support staff and the school administration. In any type of crisis, including suicide, the principal or designee is ultimately responsible for the outcomes of the building. However, they usually rely heavily on the counselor and support staff to implement the plan and support the students, the staff, and the community. There is a great deal of trust and communication that must take place between the groups when planning for and facing a suicide.

As we previously discussed, all of the stages of caring for suicide involve the administration in some manner: the suicide *prevention* program must have the buy-in and support of the administration, the suicide *intervention* program must also have the buy-in and support of the administration, and the suicide *postvention* program directly involves the principal or their designee in the planning and implementation stages. Aside from all of the involvement in these programs, there are some additional considerations for administrators. Counselors and support staff will want to continue to partner with your administrators with the following considerations.

1. **Training** – What kind of training is offered to *all* staff on a regular basis? Would they know what to do when faced with a student who is suicidal or in crisis? There are evidence-based programs that are available for training, which you'll find in the resource section of the book.

2. **Coordination** – The administration must coordinate on a much larger scale. The principal is usually the first individual to know about the death by suicide as they are contacted by the police or the assistant superintendent. Their role as a coordinator is on a macrolevel, and the support staff is able to focus on the individual needs of students and staff. Therefore, I am sharing a Care/Crisis Team Plan and a Crisis Response Manual in the resource section to help administrators proactively review some of your current practices or utilize to put a plan in place.

3. **Communication** – The administration must communicate with various groups after a death by suicide. This can be a very difficult experience for even a veteran administrator. Administrators may be contacted by media, the family who just lost their student, staff who are grieving, etc. Knowing how to communicate professionally and appropriately is critical. In the resources section, I share the following:

- A sample letter to the community
- A sample script that staff can read to their classes
- A sample flow chart for media communication

As with any of the resources that are being provided, these are tools for you to use as you develop the best suicide programs for your school and your district. I want to again stress that you must look at the needs of your student, your staff, and your community. Look at your goals and your data. Then implement a program that meets your needs.

A Staff Member's Story

Sometimes in the hurriedness of the day, we forget that our administrators are also people who are dealing with their own thoughts and feelings. This is particularly true in a time of crisis and loss. We look to our leaders to provide answers, give information, and be strong. But when do they, and when do we, get to be human?

After a third student died by suicide one school year, I walked into my principal's office. It was very early in the morning, and we planned to meet to review the crisis plan and ensure that everything was in order to again support our students, our staff, and our community. But this time something was different. The lights were low and the music was soft. My principal's back was to the door, and his jacket was thrown over his desk chair. He just sat there with his head in his hands. I knocked softly so as not to fully disturb him, but there was no reply. I continued to walk in and sit across from him in the office chair.

"Would you like to reschedule? I can get the rooms ready and then come back in an hour."

"No, I don't think I can do this again," he said. "How many more times am I going to have to do this?"

"I don't know."

We sat there in silence. That was what he needed at the time. Just to be able to sit there in silence. He wasn't worried about the plan since it had already been implemented twice earlier in the year; everyone knew what to do.

I knew in that moment that he would not come back after that school year. The deaths had taken their toll on him, and he could no longer look at students who lost their friend, parents who lost their son or daughter, and the community who lost a child too soon.

QUESTIONS to CONSIDER

1. What kind of training is offered to your entire staff on a regular basis?

2. Would they know what to do when faced with a student who is suicidal or in crisis?

3. What is the difference in roles for the principal and the support staff?

KEY POINTS

- All stages of responding to and caring for a suicide involve the administration and must have their buy-in and support.

- Ongoing suicide training is critical for administration and staff.

- Successful coordination requires that everyone knows their role.

- Knowing how to communicate professionally and appropriately with the media, the family who has lost the student, and the staff is critical.

8 Suicide P/I/P Strategies for Teachers

Alone we can do so little; together we can do so much.
—Helen Keller

Teachers and other individuals in the school building have a very important role in suicide prevention and awareness. While they will not be asked to implement a suicide intervention with a student, they do need to be able to easily identify the warning signs and risk factors and know exactly what to do when they believe that an individual is thinking about suicide. There are some ways that we, as the support staff, can make this as simple as possible for teachers. Here are some best practices that you can implement in your buildings.

1. All school staff should be trained each year (and ideally each semester) on the suicide protocol. Remind staff what they are looking for and what to do when they see/hear it.

2. Provide the staff with a simple Suicide Protocol flowchart (in the resources section of the book) that they can keep readily available.

3. Let staff know what to do if they are alerted to a suicide threat during or outside of the school day. See below and in the resources section of the book.

15-MINUTE FOCUS
Educator's Guide to Suicide Prevention, Intervention, and Postvention

4. Ask staff to remain in the classrooms when you provide the suicide prevention lessons to students. It is important for them to also learn about the program that you are implementing so that they can best support students, staff, and the school in these suicide prevention efforts.

It is important that all staff understand that they are part of the team to keep students and staff safe. It is only when the whole team functions as a single unit that you can make the greatest impact.

Suicide Protocol for Teachers

When a student shares that they are having suicidal thoughts with you or another staff member, it is important that you follow the right steps to address it.

1. When a student discloses suicidal ideations to you as a teacher, you should immediately tell the school designee (this is usually a school counselor or other support staff member).
2. The school designee should assess the risk, utilize their resources to support the student, and assist in intervention.
3. The school designee should work to create a safety plan for the student.
4. The school designee should contact the parent or guardian to provide them with resources.
5. The school should create a re-entry plan for the student.

Student Disclosure –
During and Outside the School Day

During the School Day

If a student discloses suicidal thoughts to you during the school day, have an adult take the student to a counselor or send a note with a trusted student to the counseling office requesting that a counselor come to your room immediately. Do not email or leave a voicemail for the counselor. You must get verbal confirmation that a counselor is coming to check on the student.

After School Hours

If a student discloses suicidal thoughts to you outside the school day, you should first contact your local DFCS office. Then, you should contact your principal. And finally, upon returning to the school building, you should contact the school counselor.

A Staff Member's Story

The relationships we build with the staff in our building can have a long and lasting impact. Not only is it critical that our staff understand the framework of the suicide protocol, but they also need to know that when we lose a student to suicide, the crisis team will be there to support them as well.

Taking care of staff during a student death can be a challenging task. Many of them won't let you know they are hurting. They won't come to a crisis center. Instead you will find them huddled in one another's classrooms hugging, crying, and trying to support each other.

When a student dies, we have to think about those teachers and staff who will be most impacted by the death. One of the students at my school who died by suicide did not die immediately; he was hospitalized for a few days. When he did pass, it was during the school day. My principal and I received word from the family, and we were asked not to share anything with the students and families until after the school day ended.

Luckily, we made it through the day without the news hitting social media. My principal told the teachers that we would be having a faculty meeting first thing in the morning. He felt like this would give him time to follow up with the family and get further clarification regarding their desires. This also allowed the crisis team to plan that afternoon so that we were ready for the staff and students in the morning.

However, I knew that there were a few teachers who were very close to this student. They needed the night to process the loss. With my principal's permission, I went to each of these teachers personally before they left the building for the day. I met with them one-on-one and shared the news of our student's death. They were each so appreciative that they were given the opportunity to have time to grieve and mourn before the announcement was made publicly. The next day was still challenging for everyone, but looking out for our staff who needed a little extra care made the day slightly easier.

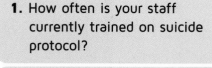
1. How often is your staff currently trained on suicide protocol?

2. Based on the Suicide Protocol flowchart, what steps should be taken when someone shares that they have had thoughts of suicide?

3. How should you respond when you hear of a threat of suicide outside of the school day? How is that different from during school hours?

4. Why is it important for staff to remain in the classroom while counselors provide suicide prevention lessons? How is that different from during school hours?

KEY POINTS

• Teachers need to be able to easily identify the warning signs and risk factors and know exactly what to do when they believe that an individual is thinking about suicide.

• School staff should be trained at least once a year on the suicide protocol and know how to respond to a threat of suicide both during school hours and outside of the school day.

• It takes the entire team working together to keep students and staff safe.

Families and Students Who Demonstrate Risk Factors

To anyone out there who's hurting, it's not a sign of weakness to ask for help. It's a sign of strength.

—Barack Obama

Families play a critical role in suicide prevention, and it is important that schools and districts partner with them in your suicide prevention efforts. One of the best ways to partner with families is through education; families who know the warning signs and risk factors for suicide are better equipped to connect their student with professional help when needed. Families can also positively contribute to the protective factors.

When an individual is experiencing thoughts of suicide, you must encourage families to take any statement they make regarding suicide seriously. This can be challenging, as families would like to sometimes excuse the statement as "attention seeking." As a partner in suicide prevention, we need all families to understand that every statement and experience will be taken seriously, and we would ask them to do the same.

As previously discussed, there are particular individuals who demonstrate risk factors for thoughts of suicide. Some of these groups include:

- Youth living with mental and/or substance use disorders
- Youth who engage in self-harm or have attempted suicide
- Youth in out-of-home settings
- Youth experiencing homelessness
- American Indian/Alaska Native youth
- LGBTQ youth
- Youth bereaved by suicide
- Youth living with medical conditions or disabilities

These students should be on your team's radar and are hopefully students you are already working with due to the nature of some of these categories. It is important to remember that these are only risk factors; there is not a direct correlation between this list and having thoughts of suicide. However, if your school or district does have a death by suicide, these are the students that your team would want to check on and connect with to ensure that they are coping appropriately.

A Staff Member's Story

When a student dies, we have to immediately begin calling the staff who will be involved in supporting the school community. My team always consisted of my school counselors. One evening, when I was making the unfortunate phone call, my colleague's wife answered.

"Hey, it's Missy. I'm so sorry to call so late."

"Let me get him for you."

"Thanks."

When he got to the phone the first thing that he said to me was "not another one."

"How did your wife know?"

"You only call the house this late with bad news." He was right. I did only call the house in the evening with bad news; I didn't want to interrupt their time as a family. I told him that I was sorry to call, but I was hoping that he could serve the same role he had during our last crisis.

This counselor had a unique talent for keeping track of the students who might need some additional support during a crisis. These might be students who had recently experienced a death in their family, had a family member die by suicide previously, had someone in their family who was terminally ill, or just needed some extra support. We could rely on this counselor to make contact with these students and families in a kind and confidential manner. He would be able to check in with them and ensure that they had the support that was needed during the new crisis. I was always grateful because this allowed me to then focus on the new crisis and the current task at hand.

QUESTIONS to CONSIDER

1. What is one of the best ways to partner with families?

2. Have you seen any of the risk factors mentioned in this chapter in any of your students? If so, which ones?

3. How can you check in on and connect with students who display any of these risk factors?

KEY POINTS

- Families play a critical role in suicide prevention, and it is important for schools and districts to work with them in suicide prevention efforts.

- You must encourage families to take any threat of suicide seriously.

- At-risk students should be on your team's radar and staff should be working with them on a regular basis.

10 Suicide Response for a Virtual Environment

Talk to people. Connect with them. Make the e-learning sound like it's a conversation between people. Real people, not robots.

—Cammy Bean

In light of recent events, we experienced suicide response in a way that was unexpected. When we were planning for the 2019–2020 school year, we did not anticipate that we would be conducting suicide postvention in a virtual platform. However, through the quarantine that was implemented due to COVID-19, our crisis response team and local care teams were asked to implement a number of suicide postvention sessions with students, staff, families, and communities.

Luckily, prior to any student deaths, my crisis coordinator and I discussed the need to implement protocol for suicide response in a virtual platform. In doing so, we wanted to ensure that we followed the same protocol and best practices that we would use if we were in a face-to-face setting. Then we would transfer these services to a virtual environment. It was critical that we were able to connect with students, staff, and the community in a manner that still felt personal. They needed to be able to have a virtual space where they could share their feelings, express their grief, and process their loss together.

Below is the guidance that was created for suicide response in a virtual setting. In addition to the information that is outlined below, it is critical to remember the following items when conducting this work in a virtual setting:

1. All participants need to turn on their cameras to show their faces. Expressions and body language can signal to staff which students are taking the news the hardest and therefore need additional support.

2. Have a staff member who is not hosting the session available to view the reactions of the participants, monitor the comments, and help with attendance. These items will be critical for follow-up procedures.

3. Debriefing after any crisis response is very important. However, it is critical in a virtual setting. The team must be able to communicate how to follow up with participants, next steps, and provide any concerns about the virtual setting that could be improved for the future for crisis response.

Virtual Crisis Response Guidance for Schools

Due to recent school closings in response to the coronavirus, we want to ensure that students and staff continue to receive grief and loss support from our district and local care teams if needed. Many of our procedures will remain the same; however, we will need to offer support services virtually for the time being.

As in the past, if a relative of a student dies, the school counselor/local care team coordinator typically reaches out to the impacted student and family members and offers additional support services. Contact and services would now take place virtually. If appropriate, the counselor would offer references from local providers. Currently many of the providers are offering tele-mental health services.

If a current student or staff member dies, the principal and/or local care team coordinator would discuss virtual crisis response with the crisis response coordinator. If extra support beyond the local care team is required, members of the district crisis team would be available to virtually join class meetings at the invitation of the principal and the local teachers, or staff meetings at the invitation of the principal. The local care team coordinator and site coordinator (principal) would determine how many classes need assistance, as well as times for scheduled meetings. The crisis response coordinator would assign members of the district crisis team to each class or scheduled staff meeting.

As in a face-to-face setting, local school counselors should follow up with highly impacted students and make referrals where needed, again making appropriate references to local providers. District crisis team leadership members are also available to schedule an individual online meeting with heavily impacted staff members and make referrals where needed.

If community debriefings are necessary, the school would offer multiple online sessions led by the site coordinator (typically the principal) and district crisis response team members; the Office of Communications and the assistant superintendent would also be involved in any community debriefings. Participants could register online in order to keep numbers manageable so that everyone attending would be able to share and ask questions.

A Student's Story

With all of the schools closed due to the COVID-19 pandemic, students were becoming accustomed to receiving invitations from their teachers to join virtual settings. But today was different. The Zoom call opened and students began to join the virtual setting. They were invited by the high school counselor and their classroom teacher earlier in the day. The students were meeting as a class, but today they would not be discussing coursework. Today they would be learning about the death of a classmate and friend.

The teacher introduced the visitors to the class: the high school counselor, the crisis response coordinator for the district, and a SEL specialist for the district. You could see the uncertainty in the small eyes of the students as you scanned the grid of participants.

The high school counselor then shared the news with the students. Based on the immediate reactions, it appeared that many of the students were hearing about the death for the first time. Tears started streaming down many of their faces. The students were then given time to share and process together.

At first, they sat silently, but then a young lady spoke up among her classmates. "I'm brokenhearted," she shared. "I don't know how to put it into words, but I always felt seen by him."

Another voice then added, "That is exactly how he made me feel. There aren't many people who really understand me, but he did."

One by one, the students began to share with each other. Although they could not physically be there to hug each other, they found ways to share love and support. They were able to communicate their grief, their guilt, and their loss.

When the session was coming to a natural close, the crisis coordinator and high school counselor shared resources for students who would like more support moving forward. The students slowly logged out of the virtual setting. When there were only a few students remaining, a student spoke up. "I was not going to join the call today. He was a neighbor, so I already knew what happened. But I feel better. Thank you." Then she signed off.

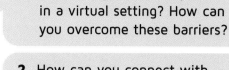

QUESTIONS to CONSIDER

1. What are the barriers to conducting suicide response in a virtual setting? How can you overcome these barriers?

2. How can you connect with students, staff, and families who need suicide response in a virtual setting?

3. What staff support would be needed to implement suicide response in a virtual setting?

KEY POINTS

- Having a plan is critical when implementing suicide related work in a virtual setting.

- You need to see the students and staff during the suicide response; ask all participants to turn on their cameras.

- Debrief with the crisis response team after the suicide work is completed and discuss how to make adjustments for the future.

Conclusion

Suicide. A sideways word, a word that people whisper and mutter and cough: a word that must be squeezed out behind cupped palms or murmured behind closed doors. It was only in dreams that I heard the word shouted, screamed.

—Lauren Oliver

As I have shared with you, there is no easy answer to dealing with suicide. There is no perfect solution for schools and school districts. Even after years of work and research in the field of suicide, there are still moments when I ask the question: "Are you thinking about suicide?" that, in the pit of my stomach, I am hoping the answer is no. But if it is not . . . if the answer is yes . . . then I know that I am prepared. That is my hope for you. I hope that the information that is shared here will help you feel prepared when a student or staff member answers yes. I want you to feel confident that you can safely help a person with thoughts of suicide, because in that moment, *nothing* else matters. And in the end, you will never know how many lives you have saved and how great your impact has truly been.

RESOURCES

DOWNLOADABLE RESOURCES

The resources in this book are available for you
as a digital download!

Please visit **15minutefocusseries.com** and click this book
cover on the page. Once you've clicked the book cover,
a prompt will ask you for a code to unlock the activities.

Please enter code:

Suicide319

Safety Plan

STUDENT NAME _____ AGE _____

SCHOOL _____ GRADE _____

PARENT/GUARDIAN OR EMERGENCY CONTACT _____

I have expressed thoughts or attempts to harm myself or others (noted below). People at my school are concerned and want to support me. I understand that I have a part in keeping myself safe.

☐ Harming Self – Ideation/Intent/Attempt

☐ Harming Others – Ideation/Intent/Attempt

☐ Other

I, _____, agree that I will not try to harm myself or others. If I think about harming myself or others, I will help myself in the following ways:

I will use these coping strategies:

1. _____
2. _____
3. _____

If the coping skills are not successful, I will:

Get help from an adult immediately:

At school, I will go to:
1. _____
2. _____
3. _____

Outside school, I will:
1. _____
2. _____
3. _____

If I am alone, I will:
1. _____
2. _____
3. _____

- **Not consume alcohol or other drugs.**
- **Not hurt myself or others.**
- **Other:** _____

CONTINUED ON NEXT PAGE

I know I can call 911 or a crisis hotline that is open twenty-four hours per day:
1. National Crisis Line – 1-800-273-TALK (1-800-273-8255)
2. Suicide Prevention Hotline – 1-800-SUICIDE (1-800-784-2433)
3. Text line: TEXTHELLO 741741

If I do not follow this plan, I understand that the following could happen:
- My parents will be contacted again.
- I will be referred to an outside resource.
- I may need to visit a hospital or treatment center.
- Other: _____

The Safety Plan follow-up date is: _____

_____
STUDENT SIGNATURE   DATE

_____
PARENT SIGNATURE   DATE

_____
SCHOOL PERSONNEL   DATE

I give permission for the identified Trusted Adults to have a copy of my Safety Plan.

Additional Notes: _____
_____
_____
_____

Key Terms

HARM TO SELF:
- **Ideation** – Suicidal thoughts without a plan/means
- **Intent** – Suicidal thoughts with a plan/means
- **Attempt** – Has actively made a suicidal attempt

SELF-INJURY
- Any attempt to inflict pain on oneself

HARM TO OTHERS:
- **Ideation** – Thoughts to hurt others without a plan/means
- **Intent** – Thoughts to hurt others with a plan/means
- **Attempt** – Has actively made an attempt to hurt others

Conference Summary

I have been informed that my child has been referred for a free assessment due to thoughts, statements, or attempts to harm themself or others. I understand that I have a responsibility to keep my child safe and, to do so, I have been advised by school personnel to take the following steps:

- Provide supervision for my child at all times and safety-proof my home. (My child should not be left alone at this time or allowed to access weapons, drugs, or medications.)
- I have been provided with a list of emergency numbers where a mental health risk assessment can be conducted.
- I have been advised to sign a release of information form so that school staff and outside professionals may share information to benefit my child.
- If my child is being assessed for self-harm/suicide risk, bring documentation of assessment by a mental health provider upon student's return to school. (See below.)
- I understand that I may be contacted by the school within 24 to 48 hours for follow-up information.
- I will notify the identified school representative when my child returns to school: _____
- In case of emergency, I should:
  1. Call 911.
  2. Call a crisis hotline and/or take my child for an immediate assessment (refer to the list of emergency numbers).
  3. Take my child to a hospital emergency room.

_____
PARENT SIGNATURE   CONTACT NUMBER   DATE

_____
SCHOOL PERSONNEL SIGNATURE   CONTACT NUMBER   DATE

Parent is to return this document to the school by: _____
                                                                DATE

To Be Completed by the Assessment Center:

_____
ASSESSMENT CENTER   DATE OF ASSESSMENT

_____
PROFESSIONAL EVALUATOR   PHONE NUMBER

Recommendations: (Check all that apply.)

☐ Inpatient Hospitalization   ☐ Group Counseling

☐ Outpatient Hospitalization   ☐ Family Counseling

☐ Individual Counseling   ☐ Other: _____

Re-Entry Plan

STUDENT   DATE

SCHOOL   GRADE

PARENT/GUARDIAN NAME(S)

PARENT/GUARDIAN CONTACT INFORMATION

REPRESENTATIVES IN ATTENDANCE

During the Re-Entry Meeting:
- Encourage the parent to stay in contact with the school about the student's treatment and needs.
- Ask the parent if the student is currently under the care of a mental health professional.
- Review any medical documentation provided by the parent.
- If needed, help to coordinate makeup work and assignments.
- Obtain signed Release of Confidential Information if the parent has not already provided this document.
- Plan with the student and parent how to handle questions about his/her absence.
- Update the Student Safety Plan if needed.
- Get permission to share the Safety Plan with the appropriate staff.

After the Re-Entry Meeting:
- If a Release of Confidential Information is obtained, consult with treatment professionals about any special needs the student may have or concerns about returning to school.
- Communicate with the teacher(s) to convey relevant, non-confidential information, answer questions, and address how the student will make up work.
- Share the Student Safety Plan with appropriate teachers, support staff, and administrators.
- Include the consulting nurse in discussion of medical/medication information (if applicable).

Ongoing Follow-Up:
- Ask the staff to monitor and report any additional concerns to the counselor.
- The counselor should check in with the student and family as needed.
- If the student has a high level of ongoing need(s) upon re-entry, refer for other support services (RTI2, social worker, school psychologist, outside mental health resources).

Additional Notes: _____

_____

_____

_____

CARE/Crisis Team Plan

The goal of the CARE/Crisis Team is to help students and staff impacted by an emergency/crisis cope and return to normal functioning in the school environment. Effective planning will enable schools to respond to the emotional needs created when an emergency/crisis occurs.

The objective is to help responders:
• Reduce pain, suffering, and inaccurate details
• Minimize disruption of daily routines at the school
• Facilitate emotional recovery of the school population through the appropriate delivery of services

The CARE Team will be comprised of the Local CARE Team (LCT) and the District Crisis Team (DCT) whose roles and responsibilities are described below:

Site Coordinator: Principal (or Designee)
• Contact Assistant Superintendent (if not immediately available, contact Chief School Leadership Officer)
• In collaboration with Assistant Superintendent, determine who will contact the Communications Office
• Communicate the school's emergency plan to the CARE/Crisis Team
• When an emergency/crisis occurs, meet with the District Crisis Response Coordinator and local CARE Team Coordinator to determine the facts and complete the Principal's Checklist and Assessment of Severity
• Communicate to parents regarding the emergency/crisis
• Communicate to teachers/staff regarding the emergency/crisis
• Communicate to students regarding the emergency/crisis (either directly or through teachers)
• Provide direction and give administrative support to the CARE/Crisis Team

School Resource Officer (SRO):
• Provide and maintain security of the building and safety for students as needed
• Secure additional community resources as needed

Local CARE Team Coordinator: Counselor at School (or Designee)
• Consult and plan with the District Crisis Response Coordinator as needed
• Work with the CARE/Crisis Team to establish a general plan and assign roles to members of the CARE/Crisis Team
• Meet with the Local CARE Team (LCT) at least once per semester to update and review your school's CARE response plan
• Designate CARE/Crisis rooms in the school for both student and staff support throughout the day. The student and staff CARE/Crisis rooms should be separate.
• Coordinate with the administrator to secure and provide written internal information for the CARE/Crisis Team (ex: script, facts, etc.)
• Provide a place for the personal belongings of the CARE/Crisis Team and plan for any needed meals
• Consult with the Principal or Designee throughout the crisis response process
• Attend the district training for the Local CARE Team Coordinator
• Facilitate support for students who need more intensive support (individual support, parent pick-up, etc.)

CARE Room Coordinator:
- Ensure that the CARE/Crisis Rooms are appropriately stocked (water, tissues, paper, pens, flip charts, crayons, construction paper, sign-in/sign-out, etc.)
- Monitor the use of the CARE/Crisis Rooms
- Communicate with the Local CARE Team Coordinator the need for additional staff

Additional CARE/Crisis Team Members (SRO, Social Workers, Psychologists, Counselor, Nurses, etc.):
- Provide student support (individual and/or group)
- Provide teacher/staff support (individual and/or group)
- Provide information on reactions to the emergency/crisis to key stakeholders
- Make appropriate community referrals

Emergency/Crisis Occurs
- Principal ensures that all students and staff are safe
- Principal completes the Principal's Checklist and Principal's Assessment of Severity

Principal contacts Assistant Superintendent
- If not immediately available, contact Chief School Leadership Officer

Principal and Assistant Superintendent determine what level of CARE/Crisis Team support (if any) is needed:
- Local CARE Team (LCT)
- District Crisis Team (DCT)

Principal and/or Assistant Superintendent contacts Crisis Response Coordinator to provide information regarding the situation and make request for assistance if needed

Local CARE Team activated at school District Crisis Team implemented if needed

Principal/Designee and CARE/Crisis Team debrief
- Summary provided to Assistant Superintendent

Principal's Checklist

- [ ] Complete Principal's Assessment of Severity.

- [ ] Gather and verify the facts by working through the campus officer or other appropriate personnel.

- [ ] ***Do not call the home. If contacted by the family, verify what the family would/would not like the school to share.

- [ ] Make determination of what level of CARE/Crisis Team intervention is needed: Local CARE Team or District Crisis Team.

- [ ] Notify Assistant Superintendent, Communications Office, and District Crisis Response Coordinator. If the Assistant Superintendent is not immediately available, contact the Chief School Leadership Officer.

- [ ] Communicate facts/plan with District Response Crisis Coordinator and Local CARE Team Coordinator (Counselor in school).

- [ ] Gather and communicate facts/plan with building staff (ex: telephone tree, staff meeting, individual contact, written).

- [ ] Communicate facts/plan with parents (ex: written, individual contact, school messenger, etc.).

- [ ] Communicate a formal statement to be read to students.

- [ ] Assign staff member to check all automated distribution lists to ensure no phone calls, mail, or notices are automatically sent to the student's or staff member's home.

- [ ] Stay in contact with the CARE Team Coordinator to ensure that everything is running smoothly.

- [ ] Conduct debriefing session with the CARE Team and/or teachers and staff.

- [ ] Communication should be approved by the Office of the Assistant Superintendent in collaboration with the Communications Office.

Principal's Assessment of Severity

1. What happened (verified with facts)?

2. Who was involved?

3. Did members of the school community witness (or cause) the incident?

4. Status of the victim? (Ex. in hospital, at home, or deceased)

5. How well-known are the people involved? (Ex. a staff member that all the students know or a student who just recently enrolled in the school.)

6. When and where did it occur?

7. Are there any family members in the school? If yes, who?

8. Are there family members of the victim(s) in any other schools? If yes, who and where?

9. Involvement of other agencies? (Ex. law enforcement, hospital, DFCS, etc.)

10. Are there other members of the school community who have a direct/ indirect connection? (Ex. clubs, sports, etc.)

11. What are the cultural needs of the students, staff, and community?

12. When did staff and students hear news of the incident? Have they had time to process their emotions?

13. What other critical events, if any, have recently impacted the school?

14. Other critical information:

Based on the responses to the above questions, the following CARE/Crisis team response is needed (can be both)

☐ Local CARE Team   ☐ District Crisis Team

When Grief Comes to School:
Protocol for School Crisis Response

The School District has a trained District Crisis Team (DCT) available to schools in the event of a death of a student, staff, or other tragic occurrence where additional support is needed. The Crisis Response Coordinator under the Student Assistance Programs department manages this team. It is comprised of school counselors, social workers, psychologists, nurses, members of the coalition of treatment providers, and other support staff.

This team is available to assist schools when a moderate to large number of students/staff will likely be grieving or emotionally upset. If the number of upset or grieving students is expected to be small (though it will still be emotionally impactful for some individuals), it may be more appropriate and a better use of resources to utilize the local school resources (school counselor, social worker, psychologist) to manage the response to a grief and loss event.

The following examples can assist in determining whether to utilize the District Crisis Team (DCT) or Local CARE Team (LCT).

WILL LIKELY NEED DCT SUPPORT	LCT MAY HANDLE
• Death of a current student • Death of a current staff member • Bus or car accident with injuries – (student or staff witnessed or involved)	• Death of a former student • Death of a former staff member or staff who has been out on leave for an extended period of time • Death of immediate family member (of student or staff member) • Death of a newly enrolled student not well-known yet

Each situation is different. It is important to contact the Crisis Response Coordinator to triage the incident. It is preferable to err on the side of caution in order to ensure the support of students and staff. Please note that grief support should always be available whether through the DCT or LCT.

Local CARE Team Planning Checklist

ISSUE	RESPONSIBLE STAFF MEMBER(S)	COMMENTS	YES	NO	YES
Obtain accurate information (re: incident)	Principal or Designee				
Contact and meet with LCT Coordinator (Counselor at School)	Principal or Designee				
Complete Assessment of Severity	Principal or Designee				
Contact Assistant Superintendent (If not immediately available, contact the Chief School Leadership Officer)	Principal or Designee				
Determine who will notify the district Crisis Response Coordinator	Principal or Designee				
Identify students and staff directly impacted	Principal/CARE Team Coordinator				
Identify students and staff with secondary impact	Principal/CARE Team Coordinator				
Provide facts and update them as needed to LCT and DCT members	Principal/CARE Team Coordinator				
Identify CARE Room location(s)	CARE Team Coordinator				
Assign CARE Team Roles	CARE Team Coordinator				
Stock Care Room(s)	CARE Team Coordinator				
Complete written statement (re: incident for staff, students, and parents)	Principal	In collaboration with Assistant Superintendent and the Communications Office			

ISSUE	RESPONSIBLE STAFF MEMBER(S)	COMMENTS	YES	NO	YES
Notify staff appropriately (ex: face-to-face in staff meeting)	Principal/CARE Team Coordinator	Not on intercom or closed-circuit TV			
Notify students appropriately	Principal/CARE Team Coordinator/Teachers	Not on intercom or closed-circuit TV			
Develop plan for providing coverage for staff who require care	Principal/Assistant Principal				
Develop protocol for students to receive additional care (ex: release slips, staff referral, etc.)	Principal/CARE Team Coordinator				
Determine if other community resources are needed	Principal/CARE Team Coordinator/CARE Team				
Determine needs of parents (ex: referral information)	Principal/CARE Team				
Set up date and time for staff and CARE team debriefing	Principal/CARE Team Coordinator				
Other					
Other					
Other					
Other					

Crisis Response Resource Manual

All schools are impacted by the realities of death, natural disasters, and even cataclysmic events at some time in their history. The District Crisis Team (DCT) is always available to assist schools in responding to such crises; however, some of the best responses come from schools where the staff has taken time to plan ahead, not only for the physical well-being of their students, but for their emotional well-being as well. This manual was developed to assist schools in both planning for a crisis and responding during a crisis. This manual is not designed to take the place of the Crisis Response Manual developed by the Safety and Security office, but rather to supplement it by providing a consistent framework for responding to the emotional needs of children and faculty at our schools in addition to physical safety issues.

Advanced Preparation for Any Event:

There are logistical arrangements that can assist in a smooth response to any kind of crisis. Making these arrangements prior to the beginning of the school year is invaluable in responding to events throughout the year.

Develop a staff phone tree/messaging system.

Deaths and accidents often occur on weekends or during the evening. Having ready access to a staff phone tree will allow the administrator to contact all faculty members prior to returning to school and give the details of the event and where and when staff should gather in the morning for a briefing on the school's response plan.

Identify a Location and Keep Supplies on Hand for a Care Center.

Care centers are locations where grieving students can come for emotional support. School counselor offices are usually too small for large groups of students. Identifying other potential locations such as group rooms, conference rooms, and empty classrooms ahead of time and making sure that they are stocked (or the counselor's office is stocked) with plenty of tissue and comfortable chairs is important. Paper bags are helpful in case a child hyperventilates. A stack of passes to return to class should be on hand as well. An optional but welcome addition is to have refreshments available for students and counselors. Grief is hard work and takes a lot of energy. Providing water will prevent people from becoming dehydrated or fainting. (Note: PTAs often want to assist in the event of a crisis, and asking them to supply refreshments is a great way to involve them in the healing process.)

Prepare a List of the Home/Cell Phone Numbers of Support Personnel.

If a death or accident impacts a large percentage of the school's population, the school counselors will need additional support. Make sure to keep the cell phone number of the Coordinator of Crisis Response or the Supervisor of School Counseling as they can activate the District Crisis Team to get additional support for your school in the event of a crisis.

Responding to Deaths or Accidents Involving Individual Students

Designate a Media Contact

Local news stations will often contact a school if a student dies or is seriously injured in

CONTINUED ON NEXT PAGE

an accident. Determine ahead of time who will take such calls. In the event of a large-scale disaster, the school district communications specialist will likely handle all media requests; however, with small scale events, the local principal may interface with the media. It's always a good idea to check in with the Office of Communications on how this should be handled.

Confirm and Prepare a Written Statement Regarding the Facts of the Death or Accident.

Prior to giving out any information regarding the circumstances surrounding the death of a student or faculty member, make sure the student's family or the police have verified the cause of death. Releasing inaccurate information can be further traumatic to the family, especially in situations that appear to be a suicide, but later turn out to be accidental. If details are missing or cannot be confirmed, staff should indicate that the cause of death is unclear at this time.

The statement can then be read by individual teachers in the classroom or by counselors that come into the class. Include information on funeral arrangements if it is available and ways students/staff can help the family through donations, cards, etc. Also include information regarding the location of the care centers so that teachers know where to send upset students.

Make sure the front office staff has a copy of the fact sheet, as concerned parents will often flood the front office with phone calls. Having a prepared statement will reduce rumors and ease parental concerns.

Hold a Faculty Meeting Prior to the Beginning of the School Day and at the End of the Day

During the morning faculty meeting the principal or designee should again share the information about the death/accident and pass out information sheets to each teacher. They should also introduce any extra counselors or support staff available and give the location of the care centers. Individual teachers can then share the information with their class first thing in the morning. **It is rarely a good idea to announce the death over the loudspeaker, as this can cause hysteria and a large exodus from class.** If individual teachers are uncomfortable sharing the information, they should be assigned a support person (school counselor or District Crisis Team member) to come to their class and share the information. In addition, classes expecting to be greatly impacted should have a counselor or DCT member accompany the teacher. Recognize that many teachers may be grieving, so make counselors or DCT members available to the staff as well.

Occasionally the student or faculty member's death is expected to have little impact outside of their own classes (for example: a self-contained child, a young elementary school child, a new student, or a child or faculty member who has been out for a long time due to illness). In such situations, the school counselor or support staff may just follow the class schedule of the student and share the details with the impacted classes rather than have all teachers share the information with their first period class.

The faculty should plan to meet again briefly at the end of the day to discuss how the day went and determine if there are additional support needs for the next day.

CONTINUED ON NEXT PAGE

Care Center Procedures

It is helpful to have some guidelines for overseeing the care of students in the care centers. A good rule of thumb is to have two counselors assigned to each group. This is especially helpful for volunteer counselors who will not be familiar with the students in their group. If someone needs to be removed, another adult will still be available to the group. It is also important not to let the group get too large—twelve students should be the maximum (space permitting). Other students who come in should be directed to a new group. It may be necessary to have several group rooms available.

Have each student sign in when they come to the care center. This will help keep tabs on who was seen and can be checked to identify students who have not been seen by the end of the day but probably need to be seen. Other students are a great source of information. In addition to asking teachers whom they are concerned about, ask students to identify other students who may have been heavily impacted, but are unlikely to come to the care center. Keep a list, and a counselor can check in with these students individually if necessary.

Students should be encouraged to return to class after spending an hour or so in the care center. Let them know that they can return later if they are having a tough time. Students who are so overcome with grief that they cannot function at school will need to have a parent come pick them up. An intervention can be accessed through the Coalition of Treatment Providers if a student appears to be extremely overwhelmed, suicidal, or self-destructive. Try to arrange a lunch break or have food brought in for the counselors. The staff is often so busy talking to students that they do not have a chance to eat.

Talking to Students about Death and Grief

Children and adolescents have very different developmental issues that come into play when talking about death. There are a variety of resources in the resources section to utilize when talking to students about grief based on their age level.

Prepare a Letter to Send Home with the Students.

Work on a letter to send home with the students (see sample letter in the resources section). This letter should include:
- What happened
- What the students have been told
- Funeral arrangements, if known
- Emotional responses parents may see in their children
- Suggestions on how to help their child
- Resources

Other Tips for Responding with Care
- Arrange for a staff member to remove the contents of the deceased student's locker (when applicable) so that they can be returned to the family.
- Do not remove the deceased student's desk or rearrange the seating without having a class discussion first, as hurt feelings may result. Discuss options with the class and decide together how to handle the empty chair.

Guidelines for Facilitating/Debriefing Small Groups

Introductory Phase
- Arrange people in a circle to facilitate processing, if feasible
- Introduce self; clarify role
- Set ground rules (issues of confidentiality, voluntary participation)
- Establish an environment of safety

Fact Phase
- Each individual introduces self and shares:
    1. What they heard about the death
    2. Where they heard it
    3. What their relationship to the deceased was
- Goal is to recreate the experience and reframe and correct misinformation
- The reality of a complex meaningful event is being described by many eyes
- Task definition: establish an experience of competence and eliminate rumors

Feeling Phase
- Begin asking feeling-oriented questions
    1. What is the worst thing about this for you?
    2. How did you feel when it happened?
    3. How are you feeling now?
- Emotional responses are acknowledged, standardized, normalized
- Provide a forum to discuss fears, anxieties, concerns
- Task Definition: group has moved from task-oriented to process-oriented
- Allow spontaneity of interpersonal support

Symptoms
- Focus on issues related to the impact of the event
- Raise questions such as:
    1. How is this affecting you physically and emotionally?
    2. What unusual things did you experience at the time of the event?
    3. What unusual things are you experiencing now?
- Explore common symptoms experienced
- Task Definition:
    - normalization of experience
    - establishing commonality
    - process of reframing and refocusing

Teaching Phase
- Educate the group (re: common stress response; discuss symptoms)
- Teach about the physiology of stress
- Present strategies for alleviating stress response
- Task Definition: establish the normalcy and adaptability of stress responses
- Provide support and direction

Summary
- Attempt to:
    1. Wrap up loose ends
    2. Answer outstanding questions
    3. Provide reassurances
- Emphasize role of communication
- Encourage use of support systems
- Suggest plans of action (appropriate memorial, scholarship fund, commemorative activities)
- Task Definition: acknowledge competence of group experience

Community Debriefing after Trauma

Separate the students from the adults, as adults will not speak freely in front of students if they feel they have to be strong. Pass out index cards so people who wish to remain anonymous with their questions can do so. Have a facilitator as well as a "floater" who can assist if someone needs to leave or needs tissues, etc.

1. Express your condolences to the group.

2. Explain some general guidelines for the debriefing. Explain that physical outbursts will not be allowed; however, they can excuse themselves if they are having difficulty and someone will check in with them.

3. Have group members share where they were and how they felt when they found out about the incident.

4. Provide education on the different feelings they may experience and physical changes such as eating and sleeping difficulties. Normalize feelings and encourage taking care of oneself physically.

5. Explain memory triggers (for example: anniversaries, birthdays, news reports) and how they may be impacted by such events.

6. Ask members to share why they think the event happened.

7. If it is a very large group, have them write down questions and pass them to the front.

8. Reassure them that it is not their fault.

9. Share community resources that are available.

What Helps People after a Traumatic Event?

- Water – helps avoid dehydration
- Exercise/Stretching
- Talking
- Tears
- Accurate Information
- Choices – Reestablish a sense of control. Do you want to sit or stand?
- Group Debriefing
- Anchoring – "This is where you can come if you need any assistance."

District Crisis Team Checklist
Creating the Plan Collaboratively with the School

The following items should be discussed with the principal and school leadership before the staff meeting:

1. Confirmation on cause of death
2. Social media challenges
3. A school designee to reach out to the family
4. What we are able or not able to say based on conversations with:
   - Family
   - District
   - Law Enforcement
   - Media
5. Parent/Guardian letter regarding the death/crisis
6. Circumstances regarding the death of student or staff
7. Notification by phone for a particular class or group
8. Locker/desk/possessions
9. Will all classes be notified of the death/crisis or just select classes/grade levels?
10. Written out script for teachers (notification and talking points)
11. Opportunity for teachers to request assistance if not comfortable sharing the script
12. Care center locations for students and staff
13. Supplies for care centers and impacted classes: tissue, water, art supplies, and Play-Doh if available
14. Plan for following the student's schedule so that counselors (school and/ or DCT) visit each class
15. Estimate on the number of DCT members needed for support
16. Planning for extra subs (if needed)
17. Planning for extra nurses (if needed)
18. Partners in ED/PTSA (food for staff during planning times)
19. Will we meet with youth leaders and club/activity leadership (if applicable) before students are told?
20. Survivor guilt possibility for both students and staff
21. Moment of silence announcement for student/staff member death (AFTER impacted students/staff have been notified)

AM/PM Staff Meeting/Mini Debrief –
Best Case/Worst Case Dealing with the Initial Shock

22. Share the plan for the day and locations of care centers
23. Rumors/social media challenges
24. Siblings/involvement/relationships

25. Identifying students and staff who may need extra support
26. Taking care of self and each other
27. Opportunity for staff to share questions/concerns
28. Follow up and possible end of day staff meeting to debrief

Sample Letter to Send Home

Dear Parents:

I regret to inform you of the death of a student who attended our school.

Jane Doe, a fourth grader, was suddenly killed by a car as she stepped off the school bus.

When we learned of Jane Doe's death, we decided to share this information with the students. It was important for all the students to have the same information to avoid rumors, which start so quickly. The facts were written down for each teacher to read to the class. Counselors and the District Crisis Team were on hand to visit each class, offering the children a time to talk and to share feelings. Students who were most upset were taken aside for individual or small group discussion. Ongoing grief and loss groups will be formed to give some of the students more time to adjust to this tragedy.

The funeral arrangements are as follows:

Cards and letters may be sent to her family at:

Our plans for a school memorial are (if known):

Your student may experience grief, and you may see some of the following emotions.
- o Tearfulness
- o Bad dreams
- o Irritability
- o Clinging to you
- o Whiney moods
- o Physical complaints—stomachaches, headaches, etc.
- o Inability to concentrate
- o A temporary dip in grades
- o More pronounced fears of dying, of the dark, of you dying, of walking home alone, etc.
- o Regressive behaviors such as reverting to thumb-sucking, bed-wetting, etc. (*include for elementary only)

Listed below are some ideas that can help your child with grieving:
- o Read a book on grief together.
- o Let your child talk about the death or draw pictures of what he or she felt happened.
- o Let them express their feelings.
- o Offer them loving, touching support.
- o Allow them to be sad and to cry.
- o Let your child ask questions and answer them as simply as you can. If you need to, it's okay to say, "I don't know how to answer that. Perhaps we can find someone who can help us.
- o Reassure your child you are healthy, you are careful when you drive, and you will be around for a long time.
- o Explain the ritual of funerals and allow their participation.
- o Offer support and structure in completing homework.

If there are any questions or concerns about your student's behavior, please call on the following:

Sincerely,

Principal

Sample Script for Teachers

Information for Students (when cause of death is not confirmed)

I am very sorry to share with you that we have some very sad news impacting our school community. We were notified yesterday that_____, a _____grade student, has died.

It's normal to feel shocked, sad, and even angry when someone we know dies. Even if you did not know _____, you may be feeling upset or sad as it can remind you of other losses.

Please be especially caring and supportive to one another today and know that you may see some students and adults crying today. This is a normal part of grief. There will also be some extra adults in the building to help.

Do any of you have any ideas of things we can do to support her family? (examples: make cards or send notes)

Do any of you have any ideas of what we can do to help support each other during this difficult time? (Listen, be supportive, give hugs)

If you need someone to talk to, we will have extra counselors available in a Care Center, so just let me or your other teachers know.

*If students ask about the cause of death, let them know that we do not have that information yet. You can ask what they have heard and mention that we have heard that too. If you feel comfortable talking about grief and loss, it is okay to allow students to share other losses they have experienced and what helped them get through the difficult times.

**If cause of death is known and confirmed, share the information in the script and process any "teachable moments" available from the cause of death (i.e. wearing seatbelts, driving speed limit, getting help for mental health/substance use issues as they are treatable diseases). Be careful not to blame. Offer messages of hope, help, and support.

Suicide Protocol

STUDENT

Student Discloses Suicidal Ideations

SCHOOL DESIGNEE

School Designee May Be the School Counselor or Other Local Support Staff

OTHER STAFF

School Staff Should Report Immediately to the School Designee

ASSESS RISK

School Designee Will Utilize Their Resources to Support the Student

ASIST INTERVENTION

RE-ENTRY PLAN

SAFETY PLAN

CONTACT & RESOURCES

School Designee Will Contact the Enrolling Adult and Provide Them with Resources

School Staff Reporting
What to Do When a Student Discloses to You

During the School Day

Have an adult bring the student to a counselor or send a note with a trusted student to the counseling office requesting that a counselor come to your room immediately. **Do not email or leave a voicemail. You must get verbal confirmation that a counselor is coming to check on the student.

After School Hours

Contact your local DFCS office.
Save this number in your cell phone.

Contact your principal.

Upon immediate return to the school building, contact the school counselor.

Media Coverage Overview Crisis Protocol

STEP ONE
Principals should secure the campus and ensure that all students and staff are safe.

STEP TWO
Principals should contact Assistant Superintendent about the event to make them aware of what is happening.

STEP THREE
Principals should conclude their initial investigation and summarize their findings with anything they find to be relevant.

STEP FOUR
Principals should communicate their summary to the Assistant Superintendents so that the district can support them with communications options.

STEP FIVE
Once facts are confirmed, principals receive district support from Communications Department and release detailed communication to their community.

What if the Media Wants to Interview/Film/Photograph Someone at the School or It Relates to the School?

For events or media requests related to students and/or staff, first contact the Communications Department for media event approval. (The Communications Department should be notified prior to media being invited on campus.) Please include name of media outlet, reporter, description of request, along with date and time if applicable.

For media interested in interviewing/filming/photographing students, the parents of the students will need to sign Permission to Allow Student to Participate in Media Relations or Interviews.

There Is a Crisis Related to My School.
How Will the Communications Department Support Me?

Please read the content dedicated to crisis communication. The main takeaway is to contact the Communications Department when a crisis arises so they can help with internal and external messaging.

References

M. Marsh, P. Agatston, A. Murphy, C. Jaffe, & J. Dess, (2018). Safety Plan. Created for the Cobb County School District.

M. Marsh, P. Agatston, A. Murphy, C. Jaffe, & J. Dess, (2018). Conference Summary. Created for the Cobb County School District.

M. Marsh, P. Agatston, A. Murphy, C. Jaffe, & J. Dess, (2018). Reentry Plan. Created for the Cobb County School District.

M. Marsh, and P. Agatston, (2020). CARE/Crisis Team Plan. Created for the Cobb County School District.

P. Agatston, and M. Marsh, (2020). Crisis Response Manual. Created for the Cobb County School District.

A. Huguelet, and M. Marsh, (2019). Suicide Protocol Flowchart. Created for the Cobb County School District.

M. Marsh, and A. Huguelet, (2019). School. Staff Reporting. Created for the Cobb County School District.

M. Marsh, (2020). Media Coverage Overview. Created for the Cobb County School District.

Trainings and Online Resources

Suicide Prevention

- Suicide Resource Prevention Center: https://www.sprc.org/keys-success/evidence-based-prevention
- Signs of Suicide: https://www.mindwise.org/what-we-offer/suicide-prevention-programs/
- Sources of Strength: https://sourcesofstrength.org
- More Than Sad: https://afsp.org/our-work/education/more-than-sad/
- The Trevor Project: https://www.thetrevorproject.org/2020/04/03/implications-of-covid-19-for-lgbtq-youth-mental-health-and-suicide-prevention/
- *A Flicker of Hope* book: https://ncyi.org/product/a-flicker-of-hope/

Suicide Intervention

- Applied Suicide Intervention Skills Training (ASIST): https://ncyi.org/product/a-flicker-of-hope/

Suicide Postvention

- PREPaRE School Safety and Crisis Training: https://www.nasponline.org/professional-development/prepare-training-curriculum
- Kate's Club Atlanta: https://katesclub.org

Crisis and Support Services

- Crisis Text Line: Text TALK to 741-741 to text with a trained crisis counselor for free, 24/7
- National Suicide Prevention Lifeline: The Lifeline is a 24-hour, toll-free suicide prevention service available to anyone with thoughts of suicide and loved ones. Call 1-800-273-TALK (8255). Callers are routed to the closest possible crisis center in their area. www.suicidepreventionlifeline.org

Online Resources

- Preventing Suicide: A Toolkit for High Schools: https://store.samhsa.gov/product/Preventing-Suicide-A-Toolkit-for-High-Schools/SMA12-4669
- After a Suicide: A Toolkit for Schools: https://afsp.org/our-work/education/after-a-suicide-a-toolkit-for-schools/
- National Center for School Crisis and Bereavement: https://www.schoolcrisiscenter.org

Notes

1. "Suicide Rising across the US," Centers for Disease Control and Prevention, June 7, 2018, https://www.cdc.gov/vitalsigns/suicide/index.html.

2. T. Dazzi, R. Gribble, S. Wessely, and N.T. Fear, "Does Asking About Suicide and Related Behaviours Induce Suicidal Ideation? What Is the Evidence?" *Psychological Medicine* 44, no. 16 (2014): 3361–3363.

3. Ibid.

4. Katy Hilts and Marion Greene, "Mental Health, Substance Misuse, and Suicide: Shared Risk and Protective Factors," The Center for Health Policy at the IU Richard M. Fairbanks School of Public Health, 18-H05 (2018): 1–16.

5. L. Dunion and L. Gordon L., "Tackling the Attitude Problem: The Achievements to Date of Scotland's 'see me' Anti-stigma Campaign," *Mental Health Today*, March 2005: 22–25.

6. Jay Asher, *Thirteen Reasons Why* (Razorbill, 2011).

7. "Suicide Rising across the US," Centers for Disease Control and Prevention, June 7, 2018, https://www.cdc.gov/vitalsigns/suicide/index.html.

8. Lindsay Holmes, L., "Why You Should Stop Saying 'Committed Suicide.' The Phrase Is Stigmatizing in a Lot of Outdated, Insensitive Ways," Huffpost, March 26, 2019, https://www.huffpost.com/entry/mental-health-language-committed-suicide_l_5aeb53ffe4b0ab5c3d6344ab.

9. Livingworks, ASIST Training Resources, https://www.livingworks.net.

10. "Suicide Rising across the US," Centers for Disease Control and Prevention, June 7, 2018, https://www.cdc.gov/vitalsigns/suicide/index.html.

11. "Suicide Statistics," American Foundation for Suicide Prevention, https://afsp.org/about-suicide/suicide-statistics/.

12. Ibid.

13. "Suicide Rising across the US," Centers for Disease Control and Prevention, June 7, 2018, https://www.cdc.gov/vitalsigns/suicide/index.html.

14. "Suicide Statistics," American Foundation for Suicide Prevention, https://afsp.org/about-suicide/suicide-statistics/.

15. "Suicide Rising across the US," Centers for Disease Control and Prevention, June 7, 2018, https://www.cdc.gov/vitalsigns/suicide/index.html.

16. Ibid.

17. Kirsten Weir, "Worrying Trends in U.S. Suicide Rates. U.S Suicide Rates Have Risen in Recent Years, While Rates in Other Nations Have Fallen. What Can We Learn from Their Examples?" American Psychological Association 50, no. 3 (2019): 24, https://www.apa.org/monitor/2019/03/trends-suicide.

18. Anne Case and Angus Deaton, "Rising Morbidity and Mortality in Midlife Among White Non-Hispanic Americans in the 21st Century, Proceeding of the National Academy of Sciences of the United States of America, 112, no. 49 (2015): 15,078–15,083, https://www.pnas.org/content/112/49/15078.

19. Kirsten Weir, "Worrying Trends in U.S. Suicide Rates. U.S Suicide Rates Have Risen in Recent Years, While Rates in Other Nations Have Fallen. What Can We Learn from Their Examples?" American Psychological Association 50, no. 3 (2019): 24, https://www.apa.org/monitor/2019/03/trends-suicide.

20. "Suicide Rising across the US," Centers for Disease Control and Prevention, June 7, 2018, https://www.cdc.gov/vitalsigns/suicide/index.html.

21. "Suicide Statistics," American Foundation for Suicide Prevention, https://afsp.org/about-suicide/suicide-statistics/.

22. "Evidence-Based Prevention," Suicide Prevention Resource Center, https://www.sprc.org/keys-success/evidence-based-prevention.

23. Ibid.

24. Ibid.

25. Ibid.

26. Ibid.

27. Ibid.

28. Ibid.

29. Casey A. Barrio Minton and Cheyenne Pease-Carter, "The Status of Crisis Preparation in Counselor Education: A National Study and Content Analysis," *Journal of Professional Counseling: Practice, Theory, and Research* 39, no. 2 (2011): 5-17, https://www.tandfonline.com/doi/abs/10.1080/15566382.2011.12033868.

30. "Listening Helps Prevent Suicide," University of Wisconsin School of Medicine and Public Health, April 28, 2009, https://www.uwhealth.org/news/listening-helps-prevent-suicide/14659.

31. Julie E. Richards, Sarah D. Hohl, Ursula Whiteside, et al., "If You Listen, I Will Talk: The Experience of Being Asked About Suicidality During Routine Primary Care," Journal of General Internal Medicine, 34 (2019): 2075–2082.

32. A. Pitman, D. Osborn, M. King, and A. Erlangsen, (2014). "Effects of Suicide Bereavement on Mental Health and Suicide Risk," *The Lancet Psychiatry* 1 (2014): 86–94.

33. K. Andriessen, K. Krysinska, K. Kõlves, and N. Reavley, "Suicide Postvention Service Models and Guidelines 2014–2019: A Systematic Review," *Frontiers in Psychology* 10 (2019): 2677.

34. Alan L. Berman, (2011). "Estimating the Population of Survivors of Suicide: Seeking an Evidence Base," Suicide Life Threat. Behav. 41 (2011): 110–116.

35. Julie Cerel, Margaret M. Brown, Myfanwy Maple, Michael Singleton, et al, "How Many People Are Exposed to Suicide? Not Six," Suicide Life Threat. Behav 49 (2019): 529–534.

36. K. Andriessen, K. Krysinska, K. Kõlves, and N. Reavley, "Suicide Postvention Service Models and Guidelines 2014–2019: A Systematic Review," *Frontiers in Psychology* 10 (2019): 2677.

37. J.L. McIntosh, "Characteristics and Effectiveness of Suicide Survivor Support Groups," *Postvention in Action: The International Handbook of Suicide Bereavement Support*, eds. K. Andriessen, K. Krysinska, and O. Grad (Göttingen/Boston: Hogrefe), (2017): 117–130.

38. G. R. Cox, E. Bailey, A.F. Jorm, N.J. Reavley, et al., "Development of Suicide Postvention Guidelines for Secondary Schools: A Delphi Study. BMC Public Health 16 (2016):180.

39. "Suicide Statistics," American Foundation for Suicide Prevention, https://afsp.org/about-suicide/suicide-statistics/.

40. Ibid.